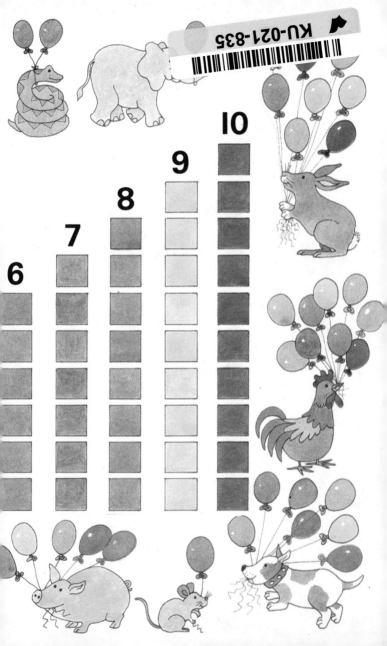

6 7 8 9 10

A simple, colourful book which encourages very young children to count objects from one to ten. Numerals and the names of numbers are introduced as well as early mathematical language such as 'biggest', 'smallest', 'same' and 'different'.

Recognising similarities and differences and talking about colours are all important pre-reading and pre-number skills. As well as enjoying the pictures in the book, repeat the activities with real objects and have fun as your child learns to count.

With very young children, we recommend that books are used with adult supervision.

British Library Cataloguing in Publication Data

Bradbury, Lynne
    Counting.—Rev.
    1. Numeration
    I. Title   II. Farmer, Lynne   III. Series
    513'.5
    ISBN 0-7214-1185-1

First edition

Published by Ladybird Books Ltd Loughborough Leicestershire UK
Ladybird Books Inc Auburn Maine 04210 USA

Printed in England

counting

by LYNNE BRADBURY
illustrated by LYNNE FARMER

Ladybird Books

one
teddy bear

2 two shoes

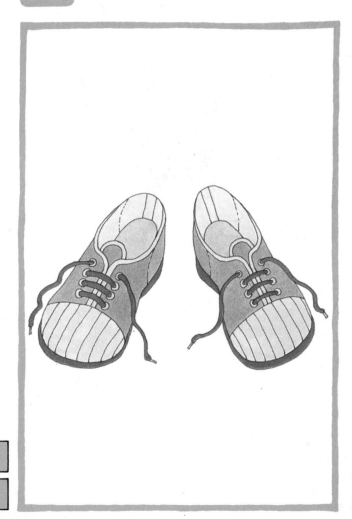

3 three kittens

4 four cars

5 five ladybirds

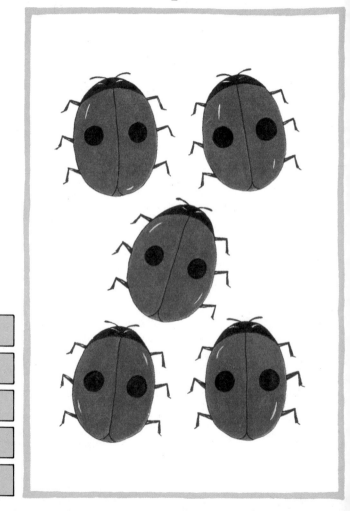

6 six fish

7 seven balloons

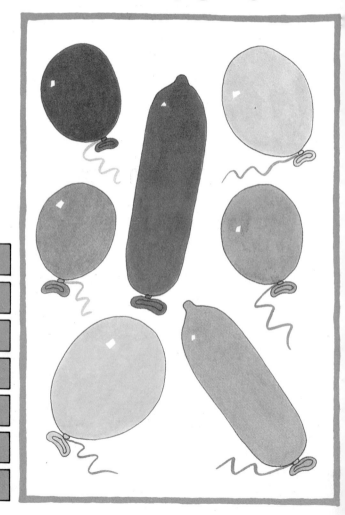

8 eight blocks

q nine flowers

10 ten buttons

How many hens?
How many eggs?

How many dogs?
How many bones?

How many flowers?
Which one is different?

How many kites?
How many blue kites?

How many socks?
Which go together?

Count these things.
Which are the same?

How many balls?
Which is the biggest?

Count the dolls.
Which is the smallest?

How many animals can catch a fish?

How many mice can have a piece of cheese?

How many green things?
How many buttons?

Count these things.
How many red
candles?

How many legs does each of these have?

Which ones have the same number of legs?

Who is first in the queue?

Ist
first

2nd
second

3rd
third

4th
fourth